Laundromat
Operations
& Maintenance
Manual

From the trenches

By

D. Rod Lloyd

Copyright 2016

Preface

Owning a coin operated Laundromat is a great business and can be very profitable. But, unless you have all new equipment, it can quickly nickel and dime you into making a loss and going out of business, losing your investment.

I write this manual not as a business major or certified appliance person [and certainly not an English major]. I write it as an average 'Joe' who bought a laundromat and needs to run and maintain the business to make an honest profit.

The skills needed to run and maintain a laundromat are not rocket science and don't need expensive equipment: just common sense and logic. And for the macho guys out there, you *will* need to ask for help from time to time.

I will assume you have no previous experience in repairing washers, dryers, change machines etc. I will get you started on a journey to taking charge of your equipment. You will get great satisfaction in making common repairs and keeping your equipment working and earning you money.

The only experience I have is what I have learned from MY machines. I do not represent to provide repair procedures for all brands, ages and types of laundromat equipment, but I will teach you how I become familiar with my equipment, their personalities, their moods and limitations. I consider this a work in progress as every week I learn something new in my 'mat'.

I do not have any problem paying for repair parts. That is the cost of doing business. What I want to avoid is the $95 service call to trouble shoot a problem by my local appliance repair company, then the part cost being doubled as their mark up and a second $95 service call to install the newly inflated part.

Even if you only make a one repair, you will save 10 times the cost of this book.

About the Author

I purchased my first laundromat in the late 1980's having made a bit of money in real estate. I was looking for something different to invest in and my local laundromat came up for sale.

It was a big store in LA and the equipment was all in good condition. Within a year we bought a second laundromat. It was a very positive experience for about 5 years but a move out of LA required us to sell.

Jump ahead 15 years. I was buying rental property but my policy was no laundry hookups in my units because they use a lot of water and besides there is a nice laundromat nearby. One day a tenant complained the local laundromat was closed. What are they to do?

I looked into it and next thing I knew, I owned it. The owner was sick of the maintenance problems and cleaning up peoples mess. It had a good income record and it was in the center of the rental units. I got it for a song.

I spent more on upgrades than the purchase price but it now is almost a full income, for just a couple hours of work a day.

Unlike my Laundromats in LA, this mat is unattended.

.

Table of Contents

Equipment Manuals

It is important to start your journey with a full set of equipment manuals. They can be downloaded for most equipment in use today from the manufacturer and many other places. At least, have them all down loaded on a computer but better still print them out and keep each in a three ring binder at your store.

These manuals tell you how to correctly install machines, their size and specifications, routine maintenance, troubleshooting and most important is the parts section. They show 'exploded' views of each area of the machine and a listing of the part name and ordering part number.

Cabinet Top and Loading Door

Cabinet Top and Loading Door

REF	PART NO.	DESCRIPTION	COMMENTS
1	33845WP	Lid	White; Painted
	33845LP	Lid	Almond; Painted
	201460WP	Lid	White; Porcelain
	201460LP	Lid and Carton Assembly	Almond; Porcelain
2	34153	Lid Plug	
3	34337	Screw	
4	503673	Screw	Optional; For added security
5	35917	Washer	Metal; Optional; For added security
6	35774	Washer	Vinyl; Optional; For added security
7	34338	Hinge Gasket	
8	52909	Screw	
9	505281	Disconnect Power Warning Label	
10	38384	Strain Relief	
11	36120WP	Top Assembly	White; Painted; Metered models
	36120LP	Top Assembly	Almond; Painted; Metered models
	36122WP	Top Assembly	White; Porcelain; Metered models
	36122LP	Top Assembly	Almond; Porcelain; Metered models
	N/A	Cabinet Top	Painted; Nonmetered models
	36273WP	Top Assembly	White; Porcelain; Nonmetered models
	36273LP	Top Assembly	Almond; Porcelain; Nonmetered models
12	27222	Nut	Optional; For added security
13	36034	Director Bracket	
14	23008	Screw	
15	N/A	Screw	
16	56534	Support Barrel	
17	36020	Nut	
18	36474	Hinge Bushing	
19	36437	Lid Hinge	Right
20	36438	Lid Hinge	Left
21	21685	Bumper	

TEST. Can you find the part number for the Right Lid Hinge and where it is on the diagram.

Once you know a part number, you can shop around the parts houses for the best price. Go to www.pwslaundry.com, enter the part number to see how much a replacement will cost.

Repair Procedure

The hardest part of maintaining your equipment is diagnosing the problem. Most of the time, replacing a defective part is a simple process of removing the mounting screw or bolt and un-plugging the wires. Then plugging the wires in the replacement part and securing it with the screws.

So how do we diagnose the problem? Well, sometimes it is pretty obvious, for example you can see if a belt is broken, water is leaking from a hose or you smell the motor has burned out. Other times it is baffling why a machine is misbehaving.

Laundromat owners have one thing going for them. We usually have a bunch of identical machines. How does this help? Most of the time, we suspect the problem is in one area. We take the most likely defective part out of the machine and replace the part from the next machine and put the suspect part in the other machine. If the troublesome machine now works and the second machine does not, you know you have found the defective part. Obtain a replacement part and install. Walla. If it does not correct the defect, try the next most likely part with the same process. Keep doing this until you track down the naughty part.

The part coming from a good machine is referred to as a 'known good' part. It is convenient to build up a stock of known good parts for testing and getting your machine back working quickly. Replace the spare part as soon as possible as problems often come back to back.

If you are not able to diagnose a problem by switching parts, the next step is to seek out help. Laundromat owners are a very sharing community. There are several forums available on the internet [example is www.coinlaundry.org]. Post a detailed description on the forum including the machine model number, and you will be surprised how many good helpful replies you will get. Chances are if you have a problem, someone else had the same problem with the exact same machine and will share how they corrected it.

Another resource is your local equipment distributor. Create a good working relationship with them. They are a gold mine of knowledge. You can also contact the manufacturer and ask for help. They frequently have repair classes you can attend and a help line.

If all else fails, contact an appliance repair company that is familiar with commercial laundry equipment. Pay them for a service call to diagnose the problem. Once the problem is found, YOU make the repair. The service person will likely have a high mark-up on the cost of the part and you will learn lots from switching the part and get the satisfaction of another success.

It is a good idea to look at YouTube to see what videos are available. Start by typing a search for 'Washing Machine Repair' and see what comes up. Watch them all if you can. It will get you mentally prepared for the challenges ahead.

Top Loaders

I will start with a typical top loader. The store I bought had 19 - 20 year old Speed Queen Washers, of which seven were not working. These machines are the gas guzzlers of our industry. They use a ton of water [well 38 gallons] and cost a lot in utilities, yet we typically charge the least for these machines. Some customers will only use top loaders.

I made the decision to replace one whole row of nine with more efficient front loaders. I chose eight MHN30 Maytag's which may not have been the best choice, I will go into later, but it gave me two working spare top loaders and [at 18 gallons per turn] reduced my utilities. The plan was to switch out any top loaders that stopped working with a working unit, keeping the machines in my store all working.

I took one of the non-repairable machines and dissected it. I took the top off, took lots of photos and notes, studied the parts and bolts and stored the working parts for spares. I removed and saved some parts off the other machines including the best machine top and fronts and took the rest to the local recycler and got some cash back for the scrap metal.

The most common problem with these old machines is the motor burning up. A new motor is $180 and in my opinion the machine is not worth putting that much money into. I looked for a used motor but they were still expensive and were sold as-is. Not worth the risk. I have since learned that local people will re-wind a motor. Do a search on line. I put an ad in my local Craig's List and was quickly contacted by a weekend warrior that will rewind a motor inexpensively.

Another problem is of course a drive belt breaking or getting burned up.  From my old machine dissection, I  understood how to replace the belt and I always keep at least one on hand.

I kept several water  inlet valves, timers and water pumps from my scrap machines.

The lid switch was troublesome on several machines. From my dissection experience, I knew how to remove the lid, install a new 'hinge bushing' which easily wear out but only cost a buck or so to replace.

The timer is an item that can malfunction. On first attempt it seems impossible to remove it. There are two bolts holding it in place. One is easily removable but the other is underneath the timer! Turns out after you remove the first bolt, the timer will slide sideways and will then come out. The wiring is connected by a large plug. Once you know how, the timer can be replaced in a problem machine in just a few minutes.

If your top loader does not stop filling, the problem will likely lie in the pressure switch or its fill tube. Refer to your parts manual. Disconnect the tube and make sure it is not clogged or damaged. If it is good, try another known good pressure switch. One or the other will likely correct the problem. If not, switch out the water inlet valve.

The first week in January I got a call from my local distributer stating they were having a year-end sale to move the last year's stock. It was a good deal so I bought 5 new top loaders model SWNBC2. They are the same size as the old machines so the install was easy. They use less water [26 gallons] and have digital controls for the customer. By this time I had used up my spare machines and still had one out of order. This left me with 4 working backup machines.

My old machines had coin slides that only went up to $2.00. We [my wife and I] were already up to $2.00 so we decided to make the old machines $2.00 for cold wash only [connected both lines to the cold faucet with a splitter]. The new machines would be hot or cold for $2.50. Most customers choose the new machines and pay the extra. This takes the strain off the older machines and I hope they last until next year's year-end sale. Some customers do stick to the old machines and they save a little money.

After four months of operation I have only had one problem with these new top loaders. A customer had put several pillows in and jammed the agitator. It burned the nylon pulley and broke the belt. That was an easy fix.

Don't be tempted to replace a belt with an automotive belt, it must be designed for that machine or it could damage the machine. Belts are designed to slip to some extent. Automotive belts might not allow this slip.

Old Top Loaders

The least profitable machine in the store will likely be the top loaders. They cost the most to run due the inefficiency and yet they are usually priced the lowest in the store. I would get rid of all of them except there is a die-hard set of customers who will use nothing else. The good news is they are easy to repair.

Unplug the Power and turn off the water supply before starting work

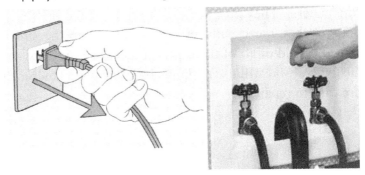

Remove two 7/16" screws at the bottom and lift off the front panel

Tip the washer back at 45 degrees for easier access

This is the Water Pump

Remove the two 7/16" screws at the front and <u>loosen</u> one 7/16" screw at the rear

Slip the belt off the pump pulley

Pull the pump out a little to access the two hose clamps [7/16" usually]. Loosen the screws and remove the two hoses.

Your pump can be removed and the replacement installed in the reverse order

Open the access door

Remove the 7/16" bolt shown. Once that bolt has been removed, the timer will slide an inch to the rear or side, then will lift out.

Disconnect the wire plug from the timer.

Remove the timer

Now you can remove the second bolt that was under the timer

With the front cover removed, remove the two 1/4" bolts holding the top. One on each side.

Remove the two Philips screws from the top of the machine

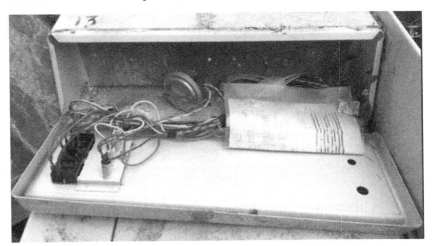

Tip the cover forward

Disconnect the pipe from the pressure switch

Disconnect the electrical connector and push them down through the hole in the top.

The top can now be removed by lifting the top front a few inches and sliding the top towards you. Watch for the lid switch that projects down by the drum.

Note how the slot in the top engages with the tab in the base

Unplug the Power and turn off the water supply before starting work

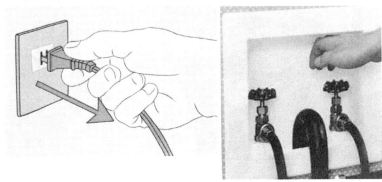

Remove two 7/16" screws at the bottom and lift off the front panel

Tip the washer back at 45 degrees for easier access

This is the Motor

Remove the four 7/16" screws, two on each side

Slip the belt off the motor pulley

Disconnect the wires at the plug

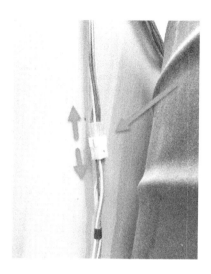

Your motor can be removed and the
replacement installed in the reverse order

The water valve is access from the rear of the machine. Remove the ¼" screw at the top. Slide the valve up to release the two tabs at the bottom.

Slide the water valve out to disconnect the hose at the top using a ¼" nut driver.

Disconnect the wire plug
and the water valve is free

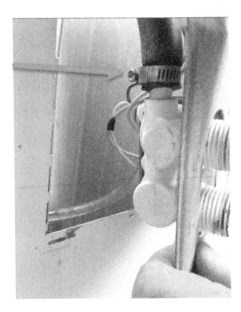

Disconnect the hose via the hose clamp

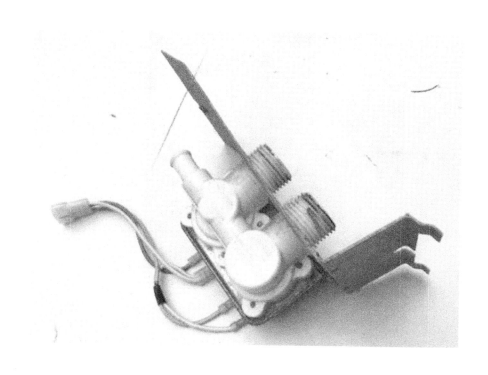

Open the mechanical door

Looking from the back, locate the coin slide [long] bolt

Undo the long bolt with a ¼" socket

Undo the Philip's screw from the Actuator [note how it is orientated]

Lift and slide out the coin slide

Maytag Front Loaders

As I said above, I replaced nine top loaders with these front loaders. They are soft mounted and pump drained units, basically a domestic machine beefed up with a coin drop added. I will explain those terms.

Soft mount means they are not bolted down. It is much better to use **hard mounts** when possible. They work better and last longer, but they are much more expensive.

Pump drain means just that, like a domestic washer, there is a pump inside the washer that discharges the water to the drain. It requires the drain to be a stand pipe and almost as high as the machine.

The alternative **gravity drain** has no pump. The machine is hard piped into the drain using gravity. There is less to go wrong with a gravity drain [socks stuck in the pump or the pump failing] and if the power fails, the water will automatically drain out and release the door. I recommend gravity drain whenever possible.

One negative to hard mount and gravity drains is the machines will need to be permanently installed which adds expense to the purchase/installation.

The model I purchased is MHN30 and the price was quite reasonable. They are a little wider than the top loaders which means I could only fit eight fronts in the place of nine tops.

The capacity is a little larger so I am not losing out on my total capacity. Also I charged more per 'turn' [one turn = one wash load] and the water usage is much less. I have owned them for six months and only had one problem.

Problem 1

That problem was a machine stopping and not releasing the door/clothes. I made a fast call to my dealer who sold the machines to me and he walked me through that solution. I needed to remove the bottom panel, reach up inside to find the door lock trip lever and bingo. Worked fine ever since.

These machines do have a couple of shortcomings.

First they do not tolerate bulky items. The larger items get water logged and the motor cannot spin the heavy load. The result is wet clothes at the end of the cycle and unhappy customers. I have warning signs on every machine about this.

Problem 2

The second problem. The machine only needs a small amount of detergent [1/8 to ¼ cup]. This smart machine detects too much soap still in the clothes and keeps repeating the rinse until the soap is gone. This is great for the customer except they do not understand why it has stopped counting down at 8 minutes for up to 20 minutes. This generates complaint calls. Also these extra rinses use a lot of my water for no additional income. More signs.

When I first installed the units, I placed them directly on the floor. The customers were almost on their knees to fill and empty the machine. The optional 2" riser they sell was not

much help. I ended up building a simple wood frame riser eight inches high and now the customer love these machines.

First remove soap drawer with a screwdriver to release the clip

Remove 4 screws

And two more screws

And remove cover

Remove two bolts

Now you can lift the top up

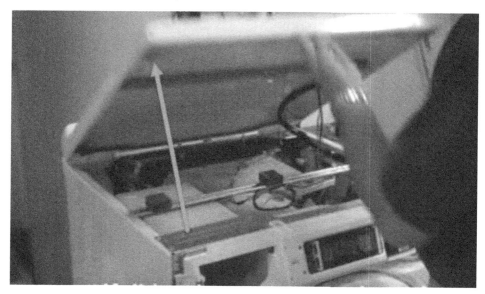

The top open

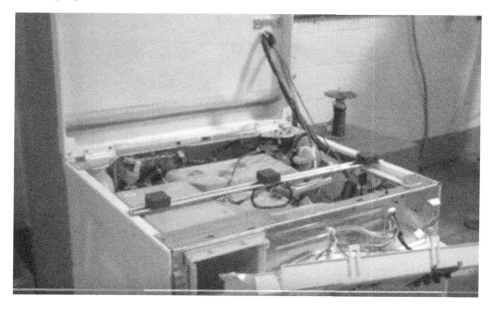

To remove the control panel

Remove 4 screws

The panel will pull forward

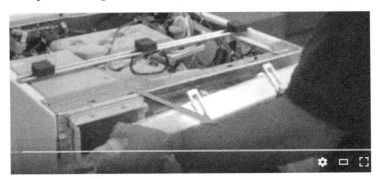

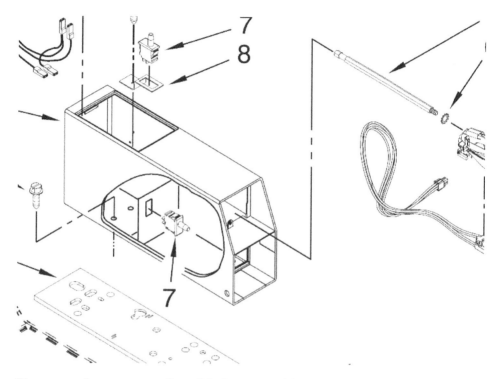

Turns out there are two [long] bolts top and bottom noted in diagram above.

Open the top access door [barrel key] and unscrew both long bolts. Stand on a stool so you can locate the end of the bolt with the nut driver.

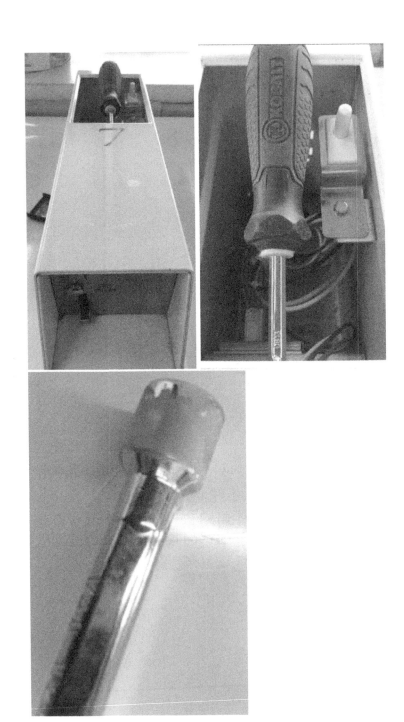

Remove the jammed item with an awl or other sharp object

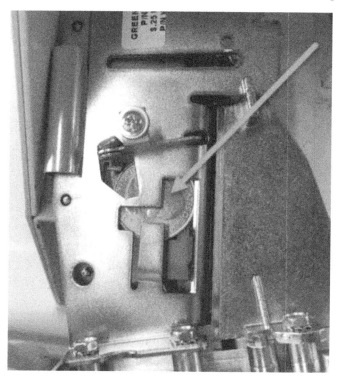

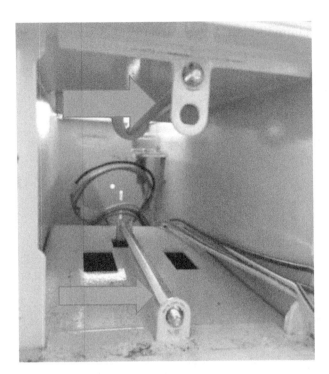

To put it back, set the long bolts in place and carefully bring the coin drop into place and secure with the nut driver. Tricky but easy after you have done it once.

Large Front Loaders

The machines look like and are heavy industrial machines. The stainless steel case is very impressive. They are of course hard mount, gravity drains and 220 volt supply. They can handle the heavy and bulky items. Each cycle is completely customizable by the laundromat owner [length of wash and spin, number of rinses, etc].

The men like to put their whole wash in a 40lb machine and let it do its thing. No sorting no nothing. The machines are very expensive to buy and install but last a lot longer than soft mount units and command a higher vend price. The moms can put a family load of lights and darks in two machines.

The spin cycle is very fast and gets the clothes dryer saving on dry time.

When I bought my store, one of the four large machines [25lb] was a total loss. It had a bad bearing, broken door glass and had been scavenged for parts by the previous owner. A second [25lb] was on its last legs. A third [40lb] was not working and took a lot to get working. The forth [25lb] was the only working machine but has loose bearings.

I searched the web and found a used reconditioned replacement 30lb machine and ordered it [SC30BC2]. We are talking about a machine that weighs 200 lb. The carrier who delivered it used a pallet dolly to place the machine right onto my base. I bolted it down, hooked up the water and electric and off it went. Even I was impressed with my handy work.

The machine I took out was studied, stripped of the valuable spare parts and recycled for scrap metal.

Problem 3

The second 40lb machine [SC40BC2] kept saying 'door not shut'. I called a repairman, Scott, recommended by my dealer. He spent several hours trying to track down the problem, [including a couple of other problems], part of this time was on the phone to the manufacturers help line. When he left it was working and I was $500 lighter. The next day I had the same door lock problem!

I called a different appliance repair company. The serviceman took one look at the machine and said "we need the company hot shot for this one". They sent out Drew and in 5 minutes it was working. All he did was lighten a wire connection to the door switch. [I got a partial refund from Scott].

Over the next few months it kept doing the same thing. Eventually, [after the experience from the next problem] I changed the door lock and the two micro switches connected to the lock and finally it is working reliably and I now know what to do with my other machines if they cause the same problem.

During the progression of this door lock problem above, a second similar 30lb machine [SC30BC2] had the same problem. Drew discovered the main circuit board was defective. Actually a 'thermistor' had blown but the manufacturer will not tell me the specs of that thermistor so it cannot be repaired. If you don't know what a thermistor is, don't worry. I don't have a clue either. [I did later, from the forum, get those specs] Drew ended up ordering a new control board which cost me $775 providing I return the old part, or $995 if I do not return the part. I did return the part begrudgingly.

With the new board installed, Drew then found the door switch was also defective which caused the control board to blow. With a new door switch installed, all is working [touch wood] and I learned everything I need to know about door locks.

I later found out I can buy a new control board for under $500, a rebuilt board for $150, or have mine rebuilt for $75. I dug out the board from the machine I scrapped, sent it to Mountain Electronics, 2880 White Oak Road, Burnsville, NC 28714 Phone 828-675-9200 who specialize in laundry electronics, and now I have a backup control board for troubleshooting and fast repairs.

The third [25lb] machine that was on its last legs, developed a coin drop problem and it leaked. A replacement coin drop was no longer available so I decided to scrap that machine after harvesting the usable parts. I found a larger 40lb machine [SC40BC2] reconditioned and new base because it was larger than

the old one.

The dealer gave me good instruction for installing the base and the machine was bolted in place. The water, power and sewer were

connected and off it went. I rented a pallet jack from a local rental place for $35, making moving the new machine into place and disposing for the old machine a breeze.

My next encounter actually inspired me to write this book. The lesson was so strong.

One of the 40lb machines had a problem: The customer reported was it was stopping mid cycle and the clothes were coming out soaking wet. To test it I put it into a cycle.

By the way, this machine can be started without coins for testing

1. Open the machine lid.
2. Locate the Program/Run switch on the computer board. This is accessed through a cutout in the metal control unit cover. This switch protrudes from the rear of the electronic control unit cover.
3. Flip the switch to the left [as seen from the front of the machine] to enter PROGRAM Mode.
4. Press the bottom right cycle button and turn off program mode. The machine will now start one cycle without putting in money.

When the cycle started it filled with water but the motor did not run. Not a sound. I checked the belt but that was fine. The motor pulley was not moving. To stop the cycle I turned off the breaker at which the drain valve should open and all the water drain out. It didn't drain out! So I seem to have two problems, no motor and no drainage. I could not understand how one would affect the other.

The next day I opened the cleanout and rooted about a foot down the pipe with a toilet auger. It appeared to be clear. I installed a blow bag and blew water through the pipe. It

appeared to be clear.

This is the machine I bought used from my local distributor. I called him and he immediately said the cause is a clogged drain. Because the machine should not be allowed to keep adding water if it does not drain, there is a little breaker inside [overload capacitor] that tripped.

I checked the breaker and sure enough the little breaker was tripped and with the press of a button, off the motor went. Next I rechecked the drain. I have my drains set up so I can dismantle the pipes easily. I removed the pipe up to the main stack and sure enough there was a sock and a bunch gunk and debris around the sock that was almost a total clog. I cleaned it out, put it back together and Walla! the machine is fine.

The moral of this story is if I had called Drew, I would have paid $95 for a service call to push a little button. He would then have told me to call a plumber to clear the clogged drain which would have cost $135 for a total cost of $230. Fact is it cost me nothing and 20 minutes of my time.

Dryers

My store came with ten 30lb, 20 year old Speed Queen Dryers [STB30XG]. Three of the ten dryers were not working.

Problem 7

The first problem machine worked intermittently. The previous owner of the laundry [who was a domestic appliance repairman], said he thought it was a bad motor. Repairman Steve checked it out and discovered the upper control board wire harness plug was not fully seated giving the intermittent problem. He reseated it in the socket and it has been fine since. This is a lesson in checking the basics first before going to more complicated scenarios.

Problem 8

The next problem machine had no heat. Steve replaced the Ignition Control and all was good. He charged me $95 for the part, which I later found I could buy for $66 at www.pwslaundry.com.

Problem 9

The third problem machine also had no heat. Steve said the spark igniter was defective and needed replacing. By now I was catching on to the part overcharge. I told Steve I would order and replace the spark igniter. It was an easy replacement and now it is working fine.

My dryers were now all working and I had learned a lot about my dryers. I now keep in stock one Spark Igniter and one Ignition Control, and can replace either in minutes.

Problem 10

 About a month later, one dryer refused to spin the

drum. I looked around the back to see if a belt had broken. I removed the protective housing and found it was chain driven by two nylon sprockets. One of the sprockets had broken. I ordered two sprockets [one as a spare] and everything worked fine. I am gaining more confidence in my abilities. I saved two $95 service call charges and the inflated part charge.

The top control panel on my machines can be removed by opening the lock, removing two screws and unplugging the wire harness. It only takes a minute or so. If I have a strange problem with a machine, the first thing I do is switch this panel with the next machine to see if the problem moves or stays with the original machine. It helps me zero in on problems.

Problem 11

I had a dryer run for about 15 seconds then stop. I started exchanging parts with no luck. I went on line and got lots of suggestions but nothing worked. Then I happen to notice the spark wire was touching the firebox. I went to move it away only to find it was melted to the box. Apparently the wire inside was touching the metal case and every time the machine called for heat, it shut the machine down. Simple fix and a reminder to look over a machine every once in a while to make sure all is good and look for the simple things first.

Change Machine

A change machine does not make you any money but if the change machine is not working, your store will slow down to a dribble of customers.

Therefore I consider this to be my most important machine in my store.

Most customers expect a change machine and without quarters they cannot use your machines.

The last thing you want them to do is to go to another local laundromat. You might lose a good customer for good.

My typical customer spends about $20 for wash and dry per week. Multiply that by 52 and you find each regular customer is worth $1,000 in income per year.

My change machine is a very old Standard Changer. It works just fine, has a large $800 coin hopper, and accepts $1, $5, $10 and $20's.

I did have one problem, I started noticing coins inside the bottom of the changer. Each time I checked the machine there were more and more coins escaping into the machine.

There was a sticker on the inside of the machine with the name of the last repair person so I was not too concerned until I called the number and they did not repair changers any more. They did not know of anyone else and referred me to the manufacturer.

I called Standard Changer and they did not have any repair people in the field. They told me to send in the hopper and they would repair it and send it back to me in about a month. Well I could not be without a change machine for a month so they put me on to the technical department. They explained it was most likely a cracked funnel.

I went to my machine, dumped out all the quarters and sure enough at the bottom of the hopper is a plastic funnel that direct the coins to the discharge mechanism. The funnel had a hole in it just large enough to allow occasional quarters to drop through.

I ordered a replacement funnel and it was a straightforward replacement process. I was still concerned that I only had one changer and at any time it could go down and be out of service for an extended period. I decided to buy a second changer.

Turns out people do not sell good used changers very often. The only units on the market were as old as mine and were very expensive. I decided to purchase a new changer.

There are two types of changer, front load and rear load. The front load units you must open the access door in the laundry for all to see and observe. This is worrying, especially when my wife goes in the changer.

The rear load machines are placed through the wall and of course you must have access from the other side. The rear load allows you to take out bills and add coins without the customer seeing anything making it much safer. I had a spot I could

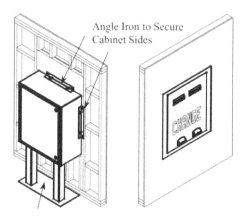

Angle Iron to Secure Cabinet Sides

install a rear load machine that would be accessed from my maintenance area and decided to purchase a MC300RL.

The rear load also has the benefit that there is very little of the machine exposed to someone wanting to break into it.

I used this opportunity to install the changer to be convenient for those in wheel chairs which my first changer is not.

ADA COMPLIANCE STANDARDS (2010)

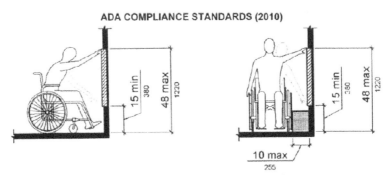

Unobstructed Forward Reach   Unobstructed Side Reach

Services

By services I am referring to the plumbing system, drainage system, electrical system and HVAC.

Unless you build a store from scratch, you inherit the infrastructure. Older stores will have aging steel water pipes, cast iron drains and who knows who installed and upgraded the electrical system.

Water Pipes

The water pipes need to be inspected to determine what material they are and what condition they are in. You then need the tools on hand to work with those pipes and parts on hand to deal with emergencies, especially replacement faucets and supply hoses.

Make sure you know where ALL the shutoff valves are and that they work easily.

Drains

Make sure you know where all the cleanouts are and at the first sign of slow drains, have a professional company root them out. The last thing you want is drains backing up on to your floor, forcing you to close the store.

Electrical

Become very familiar with your breaker panel. Each machine should have its own breaker. Make sure all the breakers are clearly marked with what it controls so you can easily shut down a machine at a moments notice.

HVAC

This could be a full central air conditioner system or a simple gas heater.

Have the system professional service at least once per year.

Security

When I purchased my store, it had no security system though there were several old security controls boxes fitted and abandoned.

I did my research. My local alarm company gave me a bid of $1,200 to install a system and $40 per month monitoring. This was too high. I knew the monthly fee was more important than the upfront cost so that was my focus in my research.

I found a company that would create a package that I would install and they would do the activation [remotely]. The equipment was either $299 with monitoring $30 per month, or $399 and $20 per month. I went with the 399/20. After 10 months it works out much cheaper.

The installation was very simple and they walked me thought the activation over the phone. The strange thing is the monitoring company is the one that quoted my $40 per month by going direct.

Lights

The lights in a laundromat need to be clean and bright. Fluorescent lights are most common, but not all fluorescents are equal. The lights are on all day and evening, often 17 hours a day, and then we usually leave some on all night.

When I bought my store, it had T12 bulbs and fixtures. T12 is the largest diameter tube, about 1 ¼ diameter. They are the least efficient strip lights.

I contacted my local electrical utility company and they sent over a lighting expert and advised me to upgrade to either T8 tubes or LED lights.

I did my research which included the cost to upgrade and the calculated savings of each option. Actually my local commercial electrical supply house did the leg work and calculations.

I would have liked to go with the LED but they are very expensive [$50 each tube] and I was worried someone would steal the tubes. I opted for the T8 tubes and new ballasts. When it was priced out, the upgrade cost was $1,100 [me doing the install] and the local utility offered me an $800 rebate in cash once it was completed. So I was only out of pocket $300 and the electrical savings paid that back in 4 months.

I suspect the cost of LED lights will drop over the next few years and might even qualify for another rebate.

While I was working with the utility guy, I asked if there were rebates for upgrading machines. He indicated yes if they are energy star rated. My eight Maytag's were and I received $800 for that upgrade. Who knew.

Surveillance

Modern technology excites me
and the concept of having
cameras in the store that could
record all the action and be
visible from my home or iPhone
was very appealing. The
problem I wrestled with is
cameras do not make you any
money. I have good insurance. They will not likely stop
vandalism etc.

In order to be able to see the cameras remotely, I needed
internet access, which would cost $30 per month. How do I
justify the cost?

I shopped around for system. I suspected they were tricky
to configure so I approached companied that specialize in
these systems. They wanted $1,500 to $2,000 and that was
not going to happen.

I researched the DIY kits and decided to proceed with the
Harbor Freight system for under $300, an 8 camera system.

I did the install which was straight forward. I now had a
monitor in the back room and a DVR recording all angles.

Next step was the remote viewing. I got an internet account
and luckily the tech department helped me with the
configuration. I would never have figured it out myself.

So, after a few months what is my feedback?

I love it. I feel so connected to my store. I know when it gets opened in the morning, I can supervise the cleaning at night and see when it gets closed.

I can observe the habits of the customer, allowing me to make adjustments to help them.

Whenever I get that call of a problem, in an instant I can see the cameras and help find solutions. When the alarm is tripped [my opening person forgetting the alarm or a broken key in one case], I can see if I need to race out the door or call the police.

Bottom line as you will guess is that it is worth every penny.

If you want to know if I would buy the Harbor Freight system again.....maybe. It is not a stellar system, but it works fine and the price was very reasonable. I feel it is a deterrent.

One day I was doing a repair to a machine. When done I gave it a test cycle. While it was running I decided to take the trash out. When I went to wrap everything up, I could not find my power screwdriver. I assumed it was under something and would turn up, but it never did. So I went to the DVR and reviewed the tape. The few seconds I was out with the trash, a young man walking by looked through the window, saw the drill, slipped in, stuck it in his jacket and out with it. The weird thing is my wife was in the store cleaning the dryer lint compartments, and never saw or heard the man. She was astonished when I showed her the tape. Lesson learned.

Tools

The number of tools needed to maintain a store is surprisingly small:

- Screwdrivers
- Wrench set
- Socket set
- Socket drivers
- Power drill/screwdriver
- Electrical tester/meter
- Hammer
- Pipe wrenches
- Vice grips
- Pliers

Chances are you will have most of these items already. I use a rolling cart. This allows me to have all the tools at hand, but easily put them out of sight when not needed. I also use this cart when I collect the coins from my machines also.

Spare Parts

You can go wild buying spare parts, and still not have what you need [or be able to find it] when the need arises. I keep my supplies to a manageable few.

- Belts
- Pump
- Switches
- Fuses
- Timer
- Water supply hoses and washers

Often, when something breaks I order two, one for the next time. Make sure you know the best laundry supply houses in your area and how long it takes to get parts to you.

Preventative Maintenance

I have always been a bit lazy when it comes to preventative maintenance. I am very observant however. I know how each machine should sound and what it should look like and I know when something is not right.

You must keep the lint compartment very clean for fire safety and operational efficiency.

Replace the water supply hoses every 5 years.

Inspect belts annually.

Clean the dryer vents annually.

Machine Optimization

By machine optimization, I am referring to keeping accurate records to allow you to make informed decisions about which machines are preferred by your customers and the cost to operate each machine to determine the vend price.

When I was purchasing my store and was discussing the income with the seller, it became clear he had little idea which machines were the most profitable or even accurately how much he was making. When he collected the money from the machines, all the money went into one bucket and was put directly into the change machine. All he knew was how much he was taking out of the change machine in dollar bills.

This is not the true measure of the income of the store. The money coming out of the machines is the true measure of income. The change machine merely changes bills to coins.

The best practice for the coin collection is to separate the income from each type of machine. In my case:

- Top loaders
- 18lb
- 25lb
- 30lb
- 40lb
- Dryers
- Soap sales

Collecting in this way, and keeping long term records, you can see which machines get the most use and plan on equipment upgrades to maximize your stores potential.

Counting coins by hand is not very practical. The two options are using a coin counter or weighing the coins. I use a commercial coin scale and gives an accurate count in seconds. I keep a spreadsheet of each collection and generate weekly, monthly and annual income reports of each item, including graphs which helps me see the trends.

From this information, dividing by the vend price you can calculate the number of turns for each type of machine and how many turns per machine per day or month. From this you can apportion utilities to each machine to determine your expenses per turn and thus how much profit a machine makes. Adjust the vent price so you make a fair profit based on your expenses for each machine.

The interior of your store needs to be attractive and welcoming. On purchasing my store the walls were painted a cold looking powder blue and in poor condition. I repainted everything a cream color. I find this to be a warm color that does not look shabby with a little wear. I keep the paint handy and touch up any problems about once per month to keep it looking smart.

I installed plenty of signs so the customer would know how much time the dryers gave for 25 cents, the size of machines and what each machine was best used for.

I installed humors signs on the wall to make it a friendly place to do laundry. I painted the concrete floor with two part epoxy garage floor paint to make it look sharp and easy to keep clean.

I have a cleaning routine to keep the store picked up and clean. All the lights are working and bright. A notice board make the place community friendly. A rack keeps reading materials neat a tidy. A few plastic flower arrangements cheer up the atmosphere. A radio helps the mood.

Attended / Unattended

My first two stores were fully attended. My current store is unattended.

There are many advantages to having a fully attended store. The staff can:

- keep the store constantly clean
- clean up spills
- security
- sell products
- advise customer
- help with problem machines
- provide wash and fold service

The problems involved in having a fully attended store are very large.

- The cost is the biggest
- Minimum wage
- Workers comp
- Hiring a service to do payroll
- Possible theft
- Staff not showing up or calling-in sick

Having done both, unless you are a very large store, I feel unattended is the better solution. Laundromats can be set up so they virtually run themselves. Customers are comfortable doing laundry without assistance and for the most part behave.

Open 24 hours

My stores have all had set hours, typically 7am or 8am to 9pm or 10pm, Your neighborhood will tell you what is appropriate for you store.

After midnight, in certain neighborhoods, the wrong crowd hang out, usually not to do laundry. This is a high risk time for little benefit to you.

The disadvantage is you must arrange for the store to be opened each morning and closed each evening which can be very time consuming for you, or an expense to pay someone else.

Closing time is a good time to pay a janitor to come in and clean everything and then close up, but finding someone to come in 7 days a week 365 days a year takes some doing.

I talked to the local police officer that works the beat in my area and he strongly advised against being open 24 hours. That is just my area and your area might be quite different.

In Conclusion

The bottom line is when you first buy a laundromat, you are embarking on a learning curve. If you are resigned to hiring all the maintenance out, you will be in for a shock. The minimum service call is going to be close to $100, plus time doing the work and parts mark up.

Also, repair people are usually busy people. It can often take a few days or even a week or more before they can respond to your problem, then time waiting for parts to arrive and another service call charge to install the new part. By servicing the machines yourself, repairs can be made very quickly. There is nothing worse than a laundromat with a bunch or machines not working. You can have pride in running your store efficiently and what a great image for the customer!

You bought a laundromat presumably to make money, now you need to run it professionally.

At first you will need help from the pro's and be asking a lot of questions, but soon you will become the master of your equipment and will be ready to pounce on the next problem. My goal is to not walk out of my store until everything is working. It is not always possible, but now you are up to the challenge.

Links

You are not on your own. You might find the following links useful for finding parts and information.

PWS [parts/manuals] www.pwslaundry.com
Speed Queen   www.speedqueen.com
Maytag   www.maytag.com
Dexter   www.dexter.com
123 Laundry   www.123laundry.com
The Laundry Forum   www.thelaundryforum.com
Coin Laundry Assoc   www.coinlaundry.org
Planet Laundry   http://www.planetlaundry.com/
Coin Wash   www.coinwash.com
Parts King   www.partsking.com
Mountain Electronics www.mountain-electronics.com
        Specialists is repairing laundry circuits boards

Notes

Made in the USA
Las Vegas, NV
23 September 2023